Transportation for the Future

Polly Goodman

Gareth Stevens
Publishing

Please visit our website, www.garethstevens.com.
For a free color catalogue of all our high-quality books,
call toll free 1-800-542-2595 or fax 1-877-542-2596.

Library of Congress Cataloging-in-Publication Data

Goodman, Polly.
Transportation for the future / Polly Goodman.
    p. cm. — (Earth alert!)
Includes index.
ISBN 978-1-4339-6011-6 (library binding)
1. Transportation—Juvenile literature. I. Title.
HE152.G56 2011
388.301'12—dc22

                          2010049263

This edition first published in 2012 by
Gareth Stevens Publishing
111 East 14th Street, Suite 349
New York, NY 10003

Copyright © 2012 Wayland/Gareth Stevens Publishing

Editorial Director: Kerri O'Donnell
Design Director: Haley Harasymiw

Printed in China

CPSIA compliance information. Batch WAS11GS. For further information contact Gareth Stevens, New York, New York at 1-800-542-2595

Picture acknowledgements
Shutterstock, cover picture; Axiom Photographic Agency (Steve Benhow) 23, (Steve Benbnw) 25, (Jim Holmes) 26; James Davis Travel Photography 20; Ecoscene (Melanie Peters) 8, 13, (John Farmar) 28; (J.C. Pasieka) 21; Foster and Partners 29 both; Hodder Wayland Picture Library (Julia Waterlow) 3, 16, 18, Impact Photos (Charles Coates) 4, (Christophe Bluntzer) 6, (Trevor Morgan) 12, (Alain Evrard) 24; Tony Stone Images (Paul Chesley) cover, (Baron Wolman) 1, (Don Smetzer) 10, (Richard Brown) 11, (David Woodfall) 14, (Will & Deni McIntyre) 15, (George Hunter) 22; (A. Black burn) 19; © Mike McGill/CORBIS 5, © Ocean/Corbis 7; © imagebroker / Alamy 9; Martin Harvey/Getty Images 21.
Artwork by Peter Bull Art Studio.

Contents

What Is Transportation?

Everybody needs transportation—to get to school or work, to go shopping, or to go on vacation. Transportation is the action of moving people or goods from one place to anothe[r]

There are many different types of transportation, from jun[bo] jets to skateboards, and from canoes to supertankers. They travel over land, water, or through the air.

Transportation and Energy

All transportation uses energy. Some uses energy produce[d] by coal or oil, such as cars, motorcycles, and airplanes. Other types of transportation use energy from the sun or th[e] wind, or from the muscles of people and animals.

Bicycles, cars, buses, and animals are all types of transportation in this Indian street. ⟳

4

Environmental Damage

Any type of transportation that is used too much can damage the environment. Too many cars produce air pollution and traffic jams, and use up the world's oil supplies. Too many walkers or mountain bikers can wear away footpaths.

Today, people are using transportation more often and for longer distances. We have to be careful about the types of transportation we use and know how much damage they cause.

↻ Skateboards are a type of wheeled transportation. The first wheels were built about 5,500 years ago.

TRANSPORTATION TIMELINE

c. 5000 BCE	Donkeys and oxen first used
c. 3500 BCE	Mesopotamians built the first wheels
c. 3200 BCE	Egyptians invented sails
1769–1813	First steam engines (trains and boats)
1880s	First gasoline engines
1903	First airplane
1920s	Cars became popular
1950s	First commercial jet airplanes
1961	First person traveled in space

Transportation without Engines

Before engines were invented about 200 years ago, the main forms of transportation were walking, sailing, or using animals. Walking and animal transportation use power made by muscles. Sailing uses power produced by the wind.

Oxen, horses, bullocks, and yaks are still used to pull vehicles and carry loads in many parts of the world today, especially on farms in poorer countries. Sailboats are also still used, but mostly for sports or fun.

Horse-drawn carts in Romania.

Bicycles

Bicycles also use energy from muscles. The muscles in our legs push the pedals, which push the wheels.

Bicycles are used for sports, such as mountain biking and road cycling. But they are also a good way to travel short distances.

Cycling is a cheap and healthy way to get around. It is also a harmless type of transportation because it doesn't burn oil to make energy.

◑ **Riding a bicycle is good exercise.**

Food Trips

Fifty years ago, most people bought food from their local store or market. Many food shops were in town centers, where people could walk to them.

Today, many supermarkets have moved to the edges of towns and cities, so people have to make car trips to buy their food.

Food can also be sent long distances to reach supermarkets.

ENERGY USE

This table shows the amount of energy different types of transportation use to travel 0.6 mile (1 kilometer).

Energy used per person to travel 0.6 mile (1 km) (in megajoules)

Car	4.23
Motorbike	2.67
Bus	0.62
Train	0.56
Walking	0.25
Cycling	0.06

Lots of foods, such as bananas, pineapples, and dates, are grown in hot countries and shipped thousands of miles to be sold.

All these journeys damage the environment. They use up a lot energy and cause pollution.

↻ Unpacking a car after a supermarket shopping trip.

TRUE STORY

BICYCLE RENTAL

In Amsterdam, the capital city of the Netherlands, around 40 percent of trips are made by bicycle. It means there are fewer traffic jams than in many cities, the air is cleaner, and the city is quieter.

There are special cycle routes across the city, separate from the streets and sidewalks. They have their own traffic-light system. This makes it fast and safe to go by bike.

Plenty of bicycle parking is provided. Train stations have huge parking lots for thousands of bikes. People can take bikes on the train, too.

A mother cycles with her children in Amsterdam. ()

Choosing Transportation

In wealthy countries, most of us can choose how to make short trips. We can walk, cycle, drive a car, or take a bus.

Sometimes cars and buses can be faster, and they can help us carry shopping and heavy bags. But if the roads are very busy, cycling or even walking can be quicker.

Many people drive cars over short distances when they could cycle or walk instead. In the United States, most car trips are under 5 miles (8 kilometers).

Safe Routes

To increase cycling and walking, countries need safe routes. Walkers, disabled people, and parents with buggies need smooth sidewalks and ramps. Cyclists need cycle lanes to separate them from traffic.

◖ Well-kept sidewalks make safe routes for everyone.

Activity

Find out how your class travel to school, using a map. Ask your teacher to help.

1. Find a map of your local area.
2. Cover the map with tracing paper and mark the position of your school.
3. Ask each class member to mark their home on the map with the way they go to school:

If they walk,
✱ draw shoes.

If they come by car,
✱ draw a car.

If they take a bus,
✱ draw a bus.

↻ **Children board a school bus in the snow.**

4. Draw lines from each home to your school and measure the distances of each.
5. Use the table on page 8 to find out how much energy each person uses to get to school.

Cars, Buses, and Trains

Cars, buses, and trains are quicker than walking or cycling. They can also carry heavier loads. Most use energy produced by burning gasoline or diesel oil. Oil is a fossil fuel that is taken from under the ground.

FOSSIL FUELS

Oil, coal, and gas are called fossil fuels. They were formed underground millions of years ago from the remains of plants and animals. Fossil fuels are being used up rapidly.

Burning oil causes air pollution and uses up the earth's energy supplies. Some experts say that if we keep on using the same amounts of oil, there will be very little left by 2040.

Trains and Trolley Cars

Some trains burn diesel oil to produce energy. Other trains and trolley cars run on electricity. Electricity can be produced by burning coal, or by using wind or water power.

Trolley cars use electricity for energy, which creates less air pollution than gasoline. ➲

Cars

Cars are the most common form of transportation in the world. More and more people own cars every day.

Cars are very convenient. They take people where they want to go, when they want to go there.

Many people choose to drive, even if they could use public transportation instead. ↻

For people who live in areas where there is no public transportation, and for some disabled people, cars are essential. Car owners can make short trips, or long trips, one after the other. Many people feel safer in cars than on buses and trains.

NUMBER OF CARS

There are about 1 billion cars in the world today. By 2015, there may be 1.2 billion.

ELECTRIC CARS

A growing number of electric cars are being produced. They run on battery power. Some can use the sun's energy to power the battery. Electric cars do not use gasoline or cause air pollution.

Damage from Cars

When cars burn gasoline or diesel, they cause air pollution, which can make it difficult for some people to breathe properly.

Cars also release gases that rise up into the earth's atmosphere. These "greenhouse" gases keep the earth warm. As we burn more fossil fuels, many scientists are worried that the earth will get hotter. If this happens, it could cause serious problems. Droughts could cause famine, sea levels could rise and cause floods, and many species of plants and animals would die.

Fumes from a car exhaust pipe. ⟲

Traffic Jams

As more and more people use cars, roads are getting busier. Many become blocked by traffic jams. In the morning and evening rush hours, traffic can stand still for a long time.

When cars stand still with their engines running, air pollution increases. So traffic jams increase air pollution.

♠ **This highway has been blocked by a traffic jam.**

Activity

TRAFFIC SURVEY

1. Ask an adult to help. Choose a busy street near your school.

2. Spend 15 minutes making a record of every car that goes past and the number of passengers inside.

3. Draw a bar graph showing your information, with a different bar for each number of passengers.

4. Which bar is longest? How could you reduce the amount of cars on the street?

Public Transportation

Public transportation such as buses, trains, and trolley cars can reduce the number of cars on roads. Each vehicle carries a large number of people, so less energy is used per person (see the table on page 8). So public transportation can reduce damage to the environment.

People will only choose to use public transportation if it is cheap, near their homes, and easy to use.

↻ A train in Argentina.

Some people think that governments should spend more money on improving public transportation than on building roads.

Beth and Mark Malallieu live with their four children in Luray, a small town in Virginia.

Mark drives 28 miles (45 km) to work every day and Beth drives 1 mile (1.6 km). Their three elder children walk to school, 5 minutes away.

Beth says: "I could cycle to work, but I have to drop Thomas off at his babysitter first. I just wouldn't feel safe coming home on a bike late at night."

Mark says there is no public transportation in their area: "There are no local buses and the nearest bus station is 20 miles (32 km) away. Everyone we know around here has a car, and most people have two."

The Malallieu family have two cars, which are used every day. ⟳

Long-Distance Transportation

Cars can be used to travel long distances, but trains or airplanes can be much quicker. They can also be very expensive.

Transporting Goods

Goods are transported around countries using trucks, trains, airplanes, and boats. Each type of transportation has a different speed, cost, and ability to carry big loads.

Boats are the cheapest way to carry heavy goods, but they are also the slowest. Trucks and trains are faster but more expensive. Trucks take goods straight to their destination.

Airplanes are the fastest transportation, but they are very expensive and not good for heavy loads.

These heavy goods are being transported on the Rhine River, in Germany. ◑

⌒ Airplane fuel
pollutes the air.

Damage from Trucks, Trains, and Boats

Boats cause the least damage to the environment.
Since they carry large loads, they use less energy for
each ton of goods.

Trucks cause the most
harm. They create air
pollution and cause
traffic jams. Since each
truck carries fewer goods
than a big boat, they
use up more energy for
each ton of goods.

PASSENGER JOURNEYS

U.S.A.

Europe

☐ Car trips   ■ Train, bus or coach   ☐ Air

19

MEASURING CAPACITY

Every road has a maximum number of vehicles it can carry quickly and safely. This is its capacity. If roads carry more vehicles than their capacity, they become congested and delays can occur.

1. Place two chairs two yards apart. This is your "road."
2. Ask four people in your class to walk quickly between the chairs as many times as possible for one minute without touching each other. Did they succeed?
3. Now increase the number of people until they start bumping into each other. When they do, you have reached the capacity of the "road."
4. Repeat the experiment moving the chairs three yards apart. Does the capacity get bigger?

Roads can be widened to increase their capacity. But this affects the local environment.

↺ **A congested street in Delhi, India.**

Developing Countries

Poorer countries have fewer roads and railroads. The only way to travel long distances is often by river, or on small airplanes. Only wealthy people can afford to fly.

TRUE STORY

TRANSPORTATION IN A RAIN FOREST

Eugenie and Jean Ivombo live with their children in a small town in Gabon, West Africa. Eugenie's parents live 236 miles (380 km) away, in the middle of the rain forest.

To visit Eugenie's parents, the family can take a bush taxi, or fly to a small airstrip in the rain forest. Driving takes 10 hours since the roads are very bumpy.

New roads are now being built in the rain forest, which could make life easier for many people in Gabon. But loggers use the roads to move in and cut down the trees. This damages the rain forest and puts animals and plants in danger.

The Ivombo family. ◑

Logs are loaded onto a truck in the Gabon rain forest. ◓

International Transportation

Most goods traveling between countries are carried by ships. Many goods are put in large metal containers and carried on container ships. Supertankers up to 1,475 feet (450 meters) long carry oil.

Since the 1960s, air travel has become much cheaper and many more people are now going abroad for their vacations. Tourists can help poor countries by bringing in money and creating jobs. Facilities such as shops and roads can be improved for local people. Tourism can help people to understand different cultures.

◖ **Many people from rich countries visit other countries on vacation.**

Damage from Tourism

Too many tourists can also cause a lot of damage. Waste from large hotels can pollute beaches and seas, destroying coral reefs and killing fish. Sports such as waterskiing and diving can also disturb wildlife.

Ancient buildings can be damaged by large numbers of visitors. Eventually, tourism can ruin beautiful places so that tourists do not want to visit them any more.

Local people can suffer from tourism, too. Tourists can change traditional ways of life and introduce foreign diseases.

∩ A polluted beach in Spain.

MEDITERRANEAN TOURISM

Every year, around 275 million tourists visit the Mediterranean region. New buildings have destroyed 75 percent of the sand dune habitats between Spain and Sicily. The World Wildlife Fund says that the loss of natural habitats means that more than 500 Mediterranean plant species are likely to die out.

23

BALI

Bali is an island in Indonesia, with a warm climate. About 3.3 million people live on Bali. Most people are Hindus, who hold religious festivals throughout each year.

In 1966, the first big beach hotel was built on the island, with running water, electricity, and elevators. Since then, many tourists have visited Bali. It is one of the most popular vacation places. Nearly 2 million foreign visitors came to the island in 2009.

⋂ A new hotel in Bali.

Builders are constantly at work on new luxury hotels, shops, restaurants, and nightclubs, and there are many new roads. Local people have made lots of money from tourism. But the island has been changed forever.

Careful Tourism

It is possible to visit other countries without damaging them. Careful tourists try not to damage the wildlife or landscape. They respect local people's cultures and try not to change them.

Activity

⋂ A lizard takes a look at some tourists in South America. The tourists are learning about the local wildlife.

HOW TO BE A GOOD TOURIST

Imagine that some children are coming to visit you. They live deep in a rain forest, on the other side of the world, where their way of life is very different.

Prepare an information pack for them about the things they will need to know. Include information about transportation, and about safety on the roads. What will they need to wear? What are the best places for them to visit? What other advice will be useful?

The Future

To protect our environment, we need to reduce the amount of energy used in transportation and develop wind and solar power to replace fossil fuels.

We should try to make few car trips to reduce air pollution and traffic jams. Car trips can be reduced if more people use public transportation, share car trips with others, and walk or cycle short distances. Governments can help by spending money on public transportation, footpaths, sidewalks, and cycle routes, to encourage people not to drive so much.

Computers and the Internet

All over the world, computers can reduce the need for people to travel and can help to reduce pollution.

There is no sidewalk for these children in Japan, so it is not safe for them to walk to school. ➲

Email and the Internet allow people to work from home instead of traveling to an office, and documents can be sent electronically using email instead of using postal transportation.

Business meetings between companies on different sides of the world can now take place using video links, which reduce the amount of air travel.

Internet shopping allows people to buy goods using their computer and have them delivered to their home, without stepping out of their front door.

⌒ Buying food at local shops is better for the environment, because it uses less energy than traveling to a shopping center or mall.

New Sources of Fuel

It is vital to encourage people to reduce use of fossil fuels. Car companies are developing electric and hybrid electric cars. Hybrid cars have an electric motor and a gasoline engine. The motor works at low speed, and the gas engine takes over at high speeds. Also, a growing number of cars are being made with solar panels. If all the electricity for electric cars was produced by power plants using solar or wind power, they would cause much less pollution.

These new inventions need to be cheap enough for all people to afford, including those in poorer countries.

This car in Australia is covered with solar panels. ⟳

Parliament Square as it is today, showing Big Ben and the Houses of Parliament. ↻

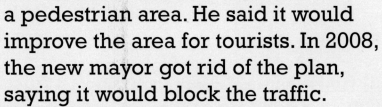

PEDESTRIAN AREA DEBATE

In the 2000s, the Mayor of London, in the UK, made plans to make Parliament Square into a pedestrian area. He said it would improve the area for tourists. In 2008, the new mayor got rid of the plan, saying it would block the traffic.

Talk about the issue with some friends and see who you think was right. Each person can choose one of the roles and talk for five minutes talking about how the pedestrian area would affect you.

* A tourist visiting Parliament Square.
* A local cafe owner.
* A disabled person who uses a wheelchair, who wants to visit Parliament Square.
* A van driver delivering to customers in the area.

↻ This photo has been altered to show Parliament Square as a pedestrianized area.

Glossary

Droughts Long periods of dry weather, or lack of rain.

Exhaust pipe A pipe underneath cars. Gases, or exhaust fumes, travel from the engine out through the exhaust pipe.

Fossil fuels Natural fuels including coal, oil, and natural gas that formed underground millions of years ago from the remains of plants and animals.

Habitat The place where particular animals or plants normally live.

Hybrid A mixture of two different things. Hybrid cars have an electric and a gasoline engine.

Megajoules Energy is measured in joules. Megajoules are thousands of joules.

Logger A person who cuts down trees for their wood.

Pedestrian areas Pedestrian areas are closed to cars. Only pedestrians, bicycles, and emergency vehicles are allowed in them.

Pedestrianize To make a road or an area only for pedestrians.

Rush hours The times in the mornings and evenings when people travel to and from work.

Smog A mixture of smoke and fog.

Solar panels Panels that absorb the sun's rays and help convert them into energy for heating or electricity.

Solar power Power produced from the sun's rays.

Supertankers Very large ships.

Wind power Energy from the wind that can be used by sailboats and to make electricity.

Further Information

Topic Web

MUSIC
- Rhythms/sounds of transportation forms
- Songs about traveling

GEOGRAPHY
- Comparing and grouping forms of transportation
- Scale of trips
- Mapwork
- Environmental, economic, and social effects
- Links between places

HISTORY
- Changing forms of transportation
- Transportation in social/economic development

ARTS & CRAFTS
- Drawing street scenes and transportation
- Postcards and travel posters

DESIGN AND TECHNOLOGY
- Designing and constructing boats, vehicles, and flying machines

MATH
- Recording, manipulating, and analyzing data
- Graphs and diagrams

SCIENCE
- Sources and uses of transportation energy
- Human body and movement
- Motion, capacity, and congestion
- Managing experiments

ENGLISH
- Using transportation as a stimulus for creative writing
- Travel poetry

Books

Tales of Invention: The Car by Chris Oxlade (Heinemann Educational Books, 2010)

Transportation: From Walking to High Speed Rail Elizabeth Raum (Heinemann Educational Books, 2010)

Do Humans Dream of Electric Cars? Your Journey to Sustainable Travel by Sustrans (Alastair Sawday's, 2009)

Websites

America on the Move
http://americanhistory.si.edu/onthemove/
Learn all about the history of transporation in the United States, from railroads to ocean liners.

Transit People
www.transitpeople.org
Discover how forms of transportation work in different cities, with pictures and lessons.

Index